Easter Bible Stories ABOUT JESUS

For 6-12-Year-Old Children

BOOKS FOR KIDS
BY MAMTALK PUBLISHING
COPYRIGHT © 2021

CONTENTS:

Introduction

When we celebrate Easter, we remember that Jesus came down to Earth about 2,000 years ago to be our Savior.

Jesus Christ and His Angels still help us and save us from sickness and problems every day!

Although we do not see them with our eyes, we can feel that Jesus and the Guardian Angel are near us.

God gives us food every day!

God gives divine support to doctors, firefighters, teachers, students, and people from all professions.

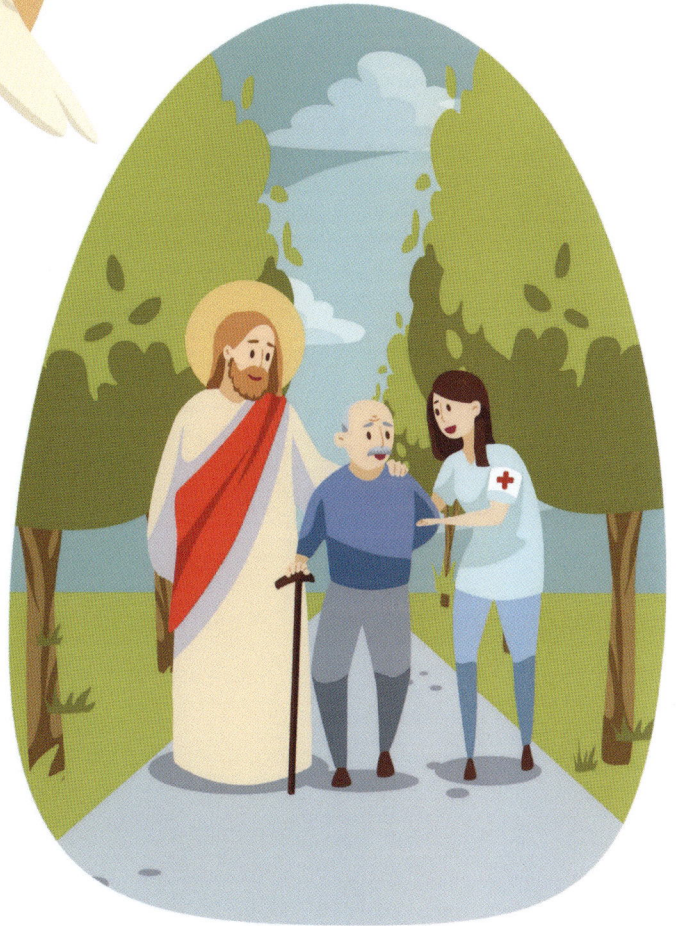

God helps with business and household chores!

God hears the prayers and requests of both children and parents!

Do you want to understand how God manages to take care of all of us?

After all, it is a real miracle that God can help everyone at the same time!

You will learn this secret from the story of Jesus during His life on Earth.

You will uncover what miracles He performed and how He died for us.

This story is the true reason why we celebrate Easter!

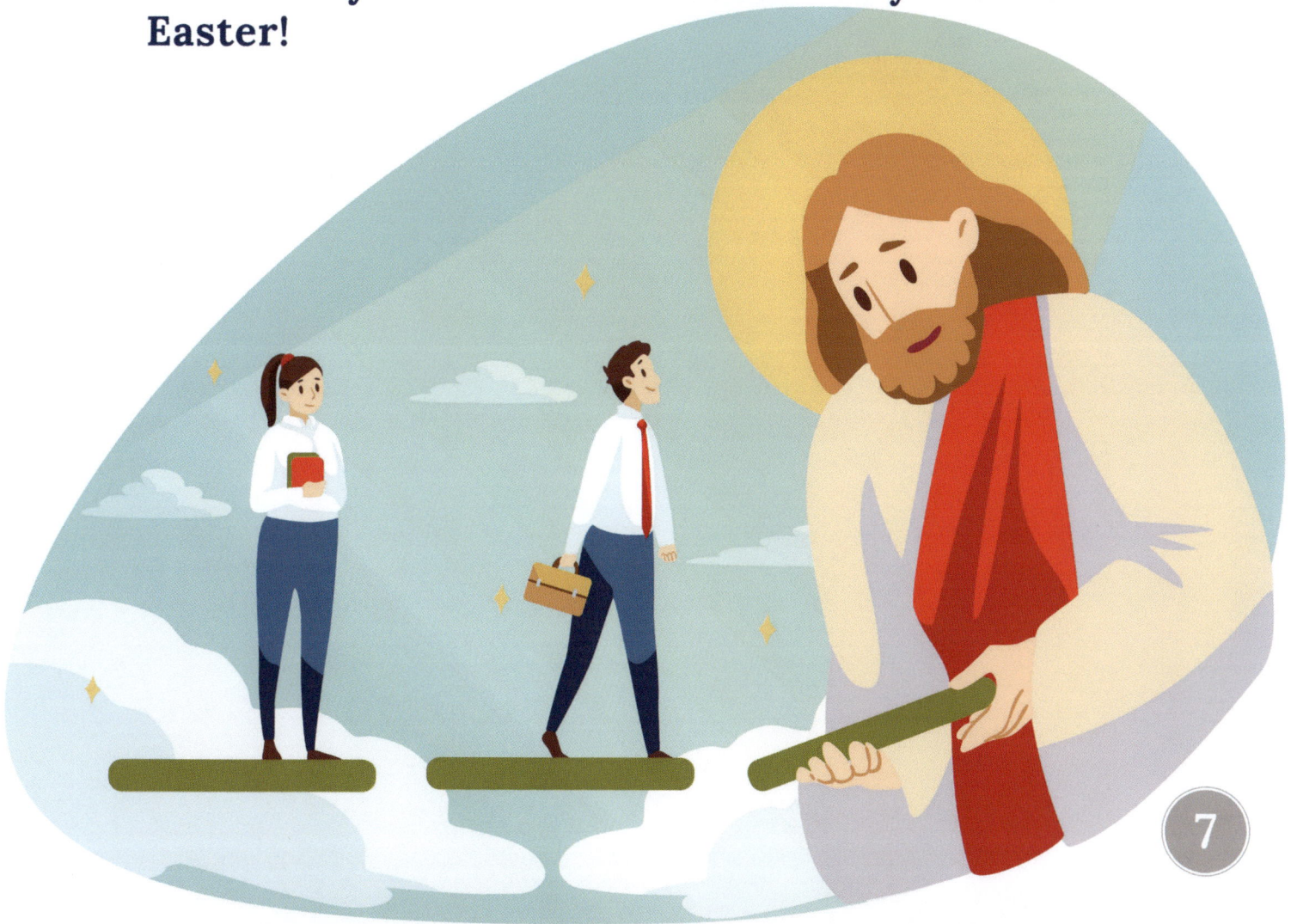

Part # 1. The Life of Jesus

Jesus was a real person Who lived on this Earth about 2,000 years ago. He was born in mysterious circumstances in Bethlehem. He grew up in Nazareth with His mother, Mary, and Her husband, Joseph.

When Jesus was about thirty years old, He started teaching people about God. He explained that He came from God and did some amazing miracles to prove it.

Jesus healed people with just one touch!

Jesus told a storm to stop, and it did!

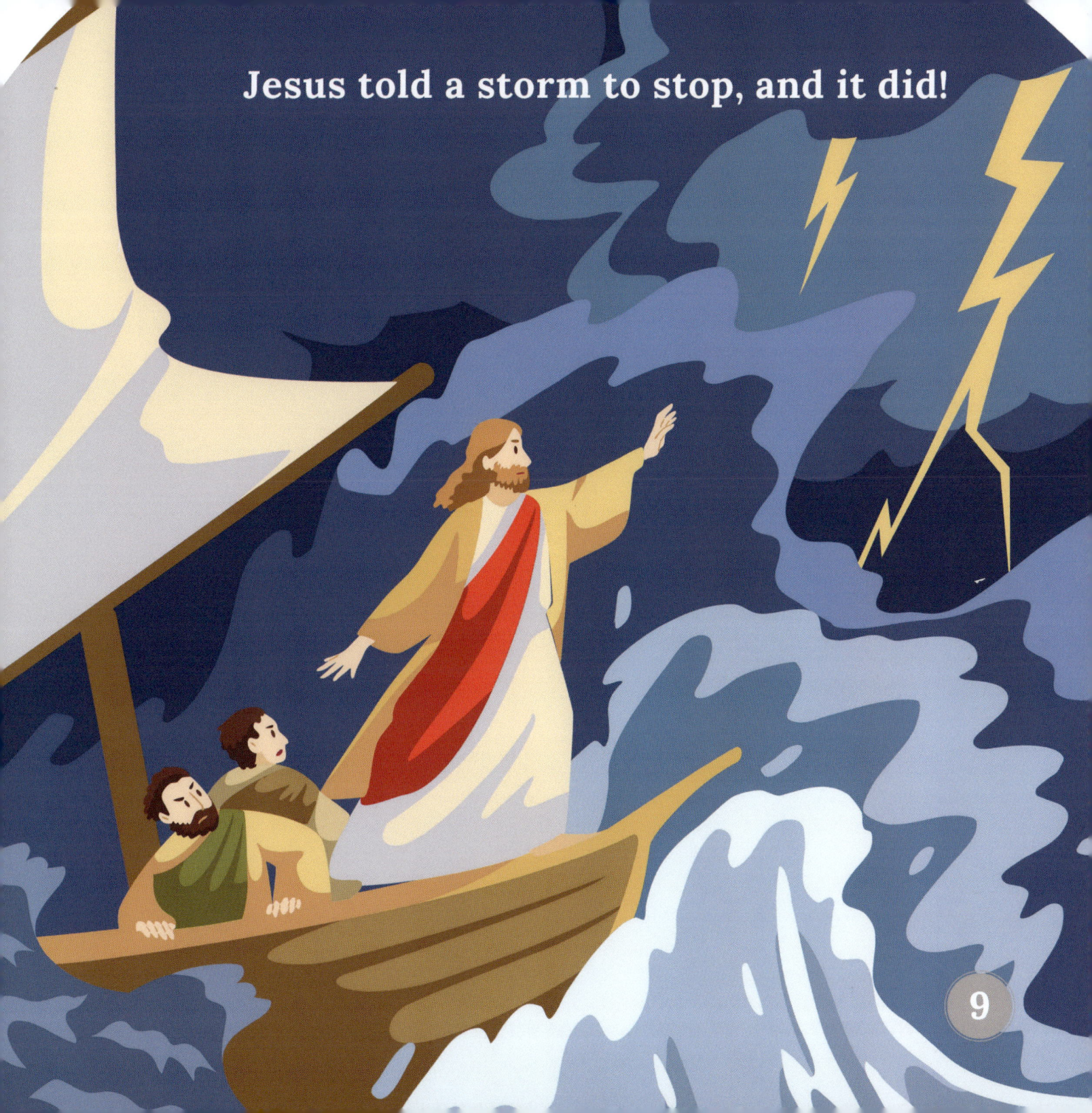

10

Jesus even raised some people from the dead!

Jesus fed 5,000 people with only
a little bit of food.

This miracle is also known as the "miracle of the five loaves and two fish." 13

Jesus performed many more miracles! He walked on water, filled the nets of fishermen with fish, and healed men who were blind!

Now you understand how Jesus feeds all the people every day – He performs the miracle again and again! Just like He fed 5,000 with five loaves!

16

Part # 2. The Entry into Jerusalem

Jesus healed people and taught them how to live according to God's law. He chose 12 people to be His disciples.

One day, Jesus and His disciples went to Jerusalem for the Passover Feast. Jesus rode into the city on a donkey. Many people remembered His miracles. They waved palm branches and shouted, "Hosanna! Hosanna!"

The leaders in Jerusalem did not like Jesus because many people followed Him.

Part # 3. The Last Supper

On Passover, Jesus gathered His disciples - the 12 Apostles for the Last Supper. Jesus knew He would leave them soon.

He washed their feet to show that He had come to Earth to serve people but not be a king.

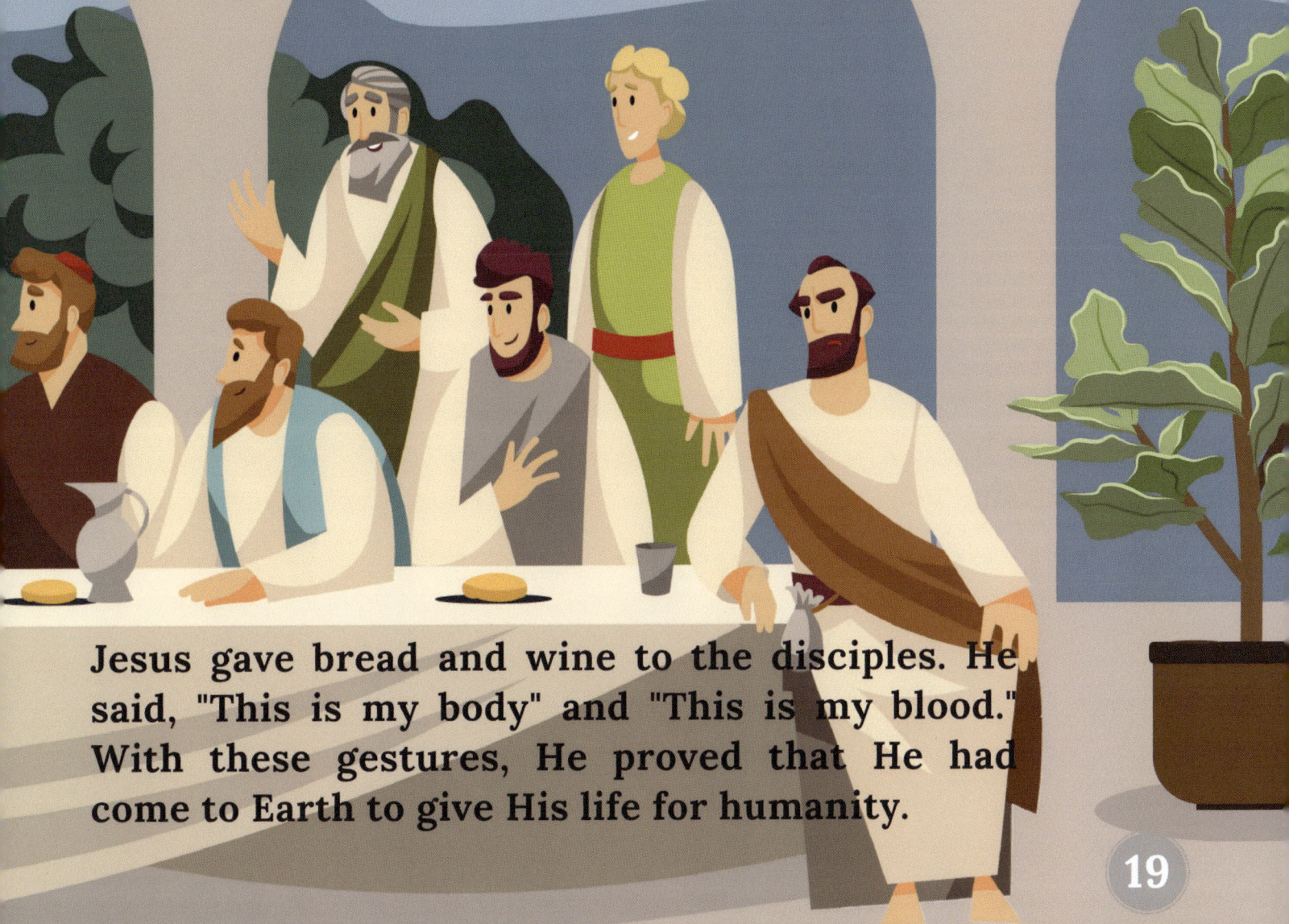

Jesus gave bread and wine to the disciples. He said, "This is my body" and "This is my blood." With these gestures, He proved that He had come to Earth to give His life for humanity.

Part # 4. Jesus Gave His Life for Us

Many people loved Jesus, which is why the leaders of Jerusalem did not like Him. They arrested Him and took Him to the Roman ruler, Pilate.

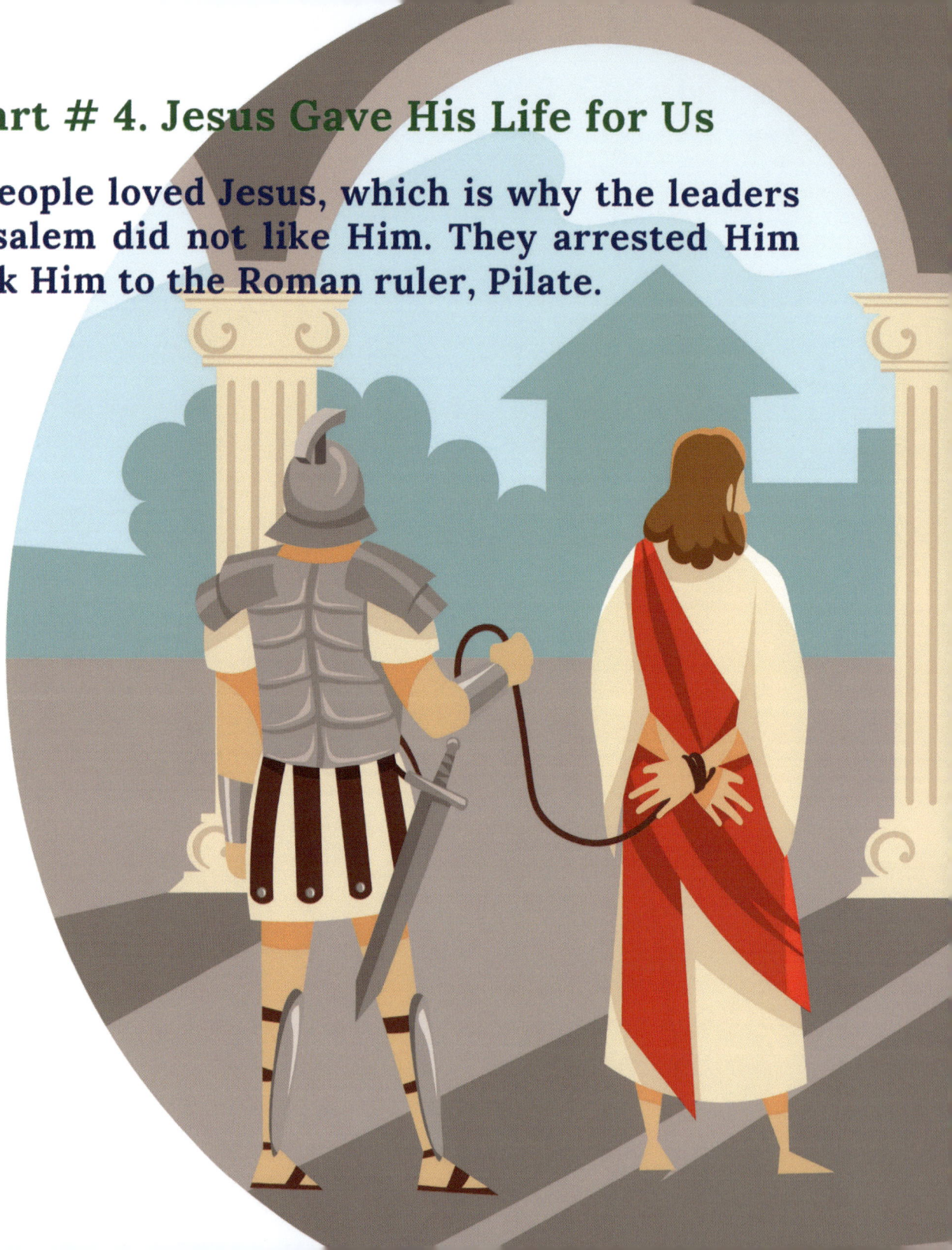

The leaders of Jerusalem told Pilate, "He said that He is the Son of God, so He must die!"

21

Pilate sentenced Him to death. The soldiers led Jesus up a hill and forced Him to carry a big wooden Cross. It was not easy, and He fell several times. Finally, soldiers put Jesus on the Cross to die.

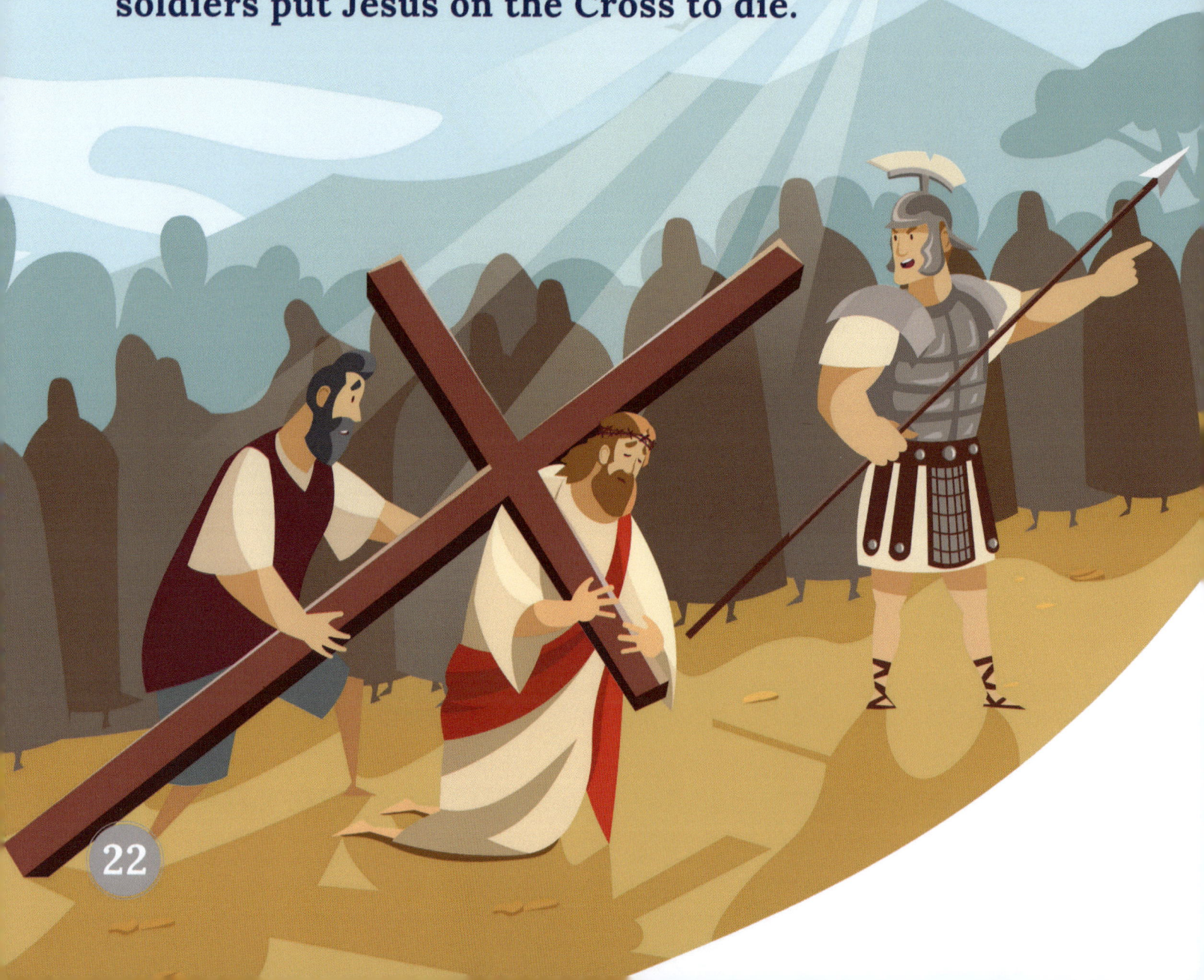

22

Jesus died on the Cross. Jesus' mother, Mary, and His disciples, who loved Him, were all very sad.

In those sad moments, they forgot something very important.

Jesus had promised He would see them again!

In fact, Jesus died but came back to life after 3 days because God resurrected Him!

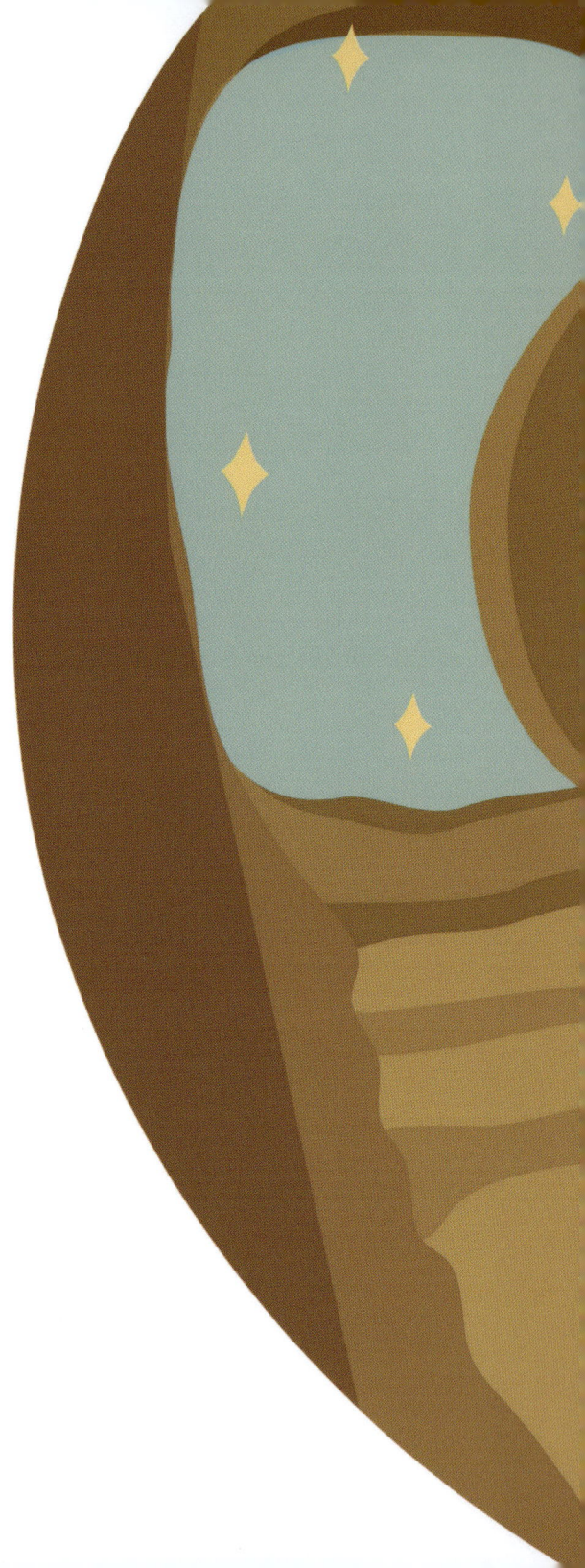

Part # 5. Ascension of Jesus Christ

Jesus appeared to His disciples - the 12 Apostles. Jesus said, "Touch my hands and feet. It is really me, and I am alive!"

The disciples were happy to see Jesus again. He said, "Tell everyone about Me. Teach them everything you learned from Me. I will always be with you!" Jesus Christ blessed the Apostles and then ascended to heaven.

The Apostles wrote down the teachings of Jesus Christ in the Gospel and passed them on throughout the Earth.

Conclusion

Dear child! Now you know why we celebrate Easter! Jesus died but came back to life after 3 days because God resurrected Him! Someday, He will return!

Jesus is the Savior of humanity! Jesus died on the Cross to pay for the sins of humanity so that we may obtain salvation! We thank Jesus for His love!

Jesus loves people very much and calls us to love all people, too! And we, like Jesus, should take care of everyone and love everyone! If someone gets sick, we will ask for this person in prayer, and Jesus and His mother, Mary, will help him!

We thank God for His love!
We thank God for His continued help!
We thank God for everything we have!

Happy Easter!

Thank you for your reading!

Happy Easter!